THE BOOK ON WEBCASTING

Dedication

To my beautiful wife,

Dina Call

for your undying support and belief
in me, even when others did not!
"I LOVE YOU!"

THE BOOK ON WEBCASTING

How To EXPLODE Your Business With Online Seminars

by Mark Call

About The Author

Mark Call was born and brought up in the state of Maine and at the time of the writing of this book still resides there with his beautiful wife Dina and their 4 children. (Marky, Brandon, Hazen & Jensyn)

Mark was raised in an entrepreneurial lifestyle. His mom and dad (Will & Suzanne Call) have always been hard working and successful business owners.

Mark grew up working for the "family" business in Maine, which went from nothing to a multi-corporation, multi-million dollar per year success story.

Mark still has his stake in the family businesses and works along side of his wife, his brother, Bill Call, and Dad on a daily basis.

He started in the *"Home Business"* industry more than 20 years ago. After many failures and "some" success, Mark turned to the Internet in 1995. Being part of the progression of high tech with a high personal touch, it is no-wonder this book became a reality.

Mark stated, *"It's amazing to think of how far we have come in a few short years with webcasting. To be part of something huge* (webcasting) *from the beginning, and know that you are a pioneer of how it shapes into the future is very humbling!"*

Despite *others* opinion, Mark never gave up on his dream of becoming a well know Internet Marketing Coach and On-Line Business Advisor. He stated it was because of (in his words) *"My wife's belief in me and un-dyeing support!"*

Today, Mark is a highly sought after Guest Presenter, Trainer and Motivational Speaker. He personally holds a minimum of two, no-cost, one hour webcasts per week, teaching others the art of webcasting and internet marketing. He does this for free as a way to "Give Back" just a little to an industry that has done so much for him.

Mark recently launched his new membership website, WebcastRiches.com. This site takes people by the hand with a blueprint "system" for success as a webcaster using the power of live broadcasting on-line. It is for those who want to truly take it to the next level with their webcasting and will evolve as the webcasting technology does.

Mark really considers Webcasting an *Art* and wants to help shape the future of Webcasting World and technology that will never go away.

One of Mark's most famous quotes is actually a question –

One year from now you will be saying one of two things… "I Wish I had"… or …

"I am Glad I did!"

- What will YOU be saying?

We hope you enjoy **"The Book on Webcasting!"**

Foreword

by Frank Sousa

I was one of the early pioneers to be running a business over the Internet. I've been doing Internet Marketing for over 12 years now... and I love it.

But if the truth be known, I am NOT a technological person, I am an IDEAS guy.

I've created several very popular software programs, and I'm probably best known for co-creating Traffic Geyser, a simple solution for uploading videos to over 120 video hosting sites with the click of a button.

My latest creation is EasyMoneyBots, a simple software system that let's your message get spread out to thousands and even hundreds of thousands of readers easily and quickly.

I have become well known all over the World and respected for my no frills approach to marketing on line and helping others put their ideas to work for them.

It has and still is a "humbling" journey. It's a journey that I would not change for anything.

I've travelled internationally speaking about how to earn money online. I've shared the stage with most of the well known "gurus" in our industry, and I've had the opportunity to meet and work with some amazing and wonderful people.

At the top of that list of amazing and wonderful people is Mark Call. I met Mark many years ago, before he was a recognized name on the internet.

Our relationship has grown tremendously, and today, I am blessed to have Mark and his beautiful wife Dina as lifelong friends.

When it comes to live Webcasting, nobody knows it better than Mark. It's something I was not used to. I turned to Mark to help me get my webcasts off the ground .... and my-oh-my what a difference it's made with my relationship to my customers.

It helps me to get across technical details quickly and easily, and helps my customers to see me as a REAL person, not just words on a page.

If you're not using Webcasting in your business, you MUST read this book...

If you ARE using Webcasting, you MUST read this book... you'll pick up a lot of POWERFUL techniques and ideas from the Master of Webcasting, Mark Call.

- Frank Sousa

xii

Acknowledgements

I wish I could take credit for this entire book and the methods that you will soon learn within, however, there are many people that influenced me and guided me to the success that I have attained in the Webcasting and Internet World.

I would like to acknowledge just a few people with a "SPECIAL THANKS"!

Dina Call - (My Wonderful Wife) whom I would be NOTHING without. Her support is like no other. I love you with everything I am...... & .... "*I AM BECAUSE OF YOU!*"

Our Great Children - (Marky, Brandon, Hazen and Jensyn) for sacrificing "time with Dad" that could never be given back for our future success. I promise it will be worth it!

Will & Suzanne Call - (My Parents) who taught me how to have an entrepreneurial spirit and to give 110% at all times. Thank you for giving me a great life.

Bill Call - (My only sibling) for putting up with some of my crazy ideas but always saying "*He will hit it big.... someday*" .....

Ken Hammond (*The Marketing Maverick*) for being a great business partner, super friend and teaming up to do over 300 webcasts with me along this journey. T.A.G. Team, bro!

Mike Potvin - for allowing me to call you at 1 A.M. and actually answering the phone. Brainstorming ideas with such a good friend is priceless. Thank you for your great friendship and support. This is truly what it is all about, brother! Meet you on the Lido deck.

Joel Therien - for allowing me to become an affiliate trainer, spokesperson and instrumental part in **his** Company to help shape the future of webcasting software and how people use it World Wide. Dude, you nailed it! More importantly, your friendship has impacted my life in such a positive way.

Josh Andrus - for giving a new meaning to "When the Student Becomes the Teacher". You are a huge success, my friend!

Frank Sousa - God blessed me for bringing Frank into my life and his friendship has guided me to the right path. To me, Frank is the true Godfather of Internet Marketing. Thank you for ALL you do for me and this entire Industry!

James Allen - my Product Advisor. I would not have been able to put it all together without you, buddy! We have only just begun!

Jason Fladien - for having great content that helped shape the direction of this book. You will go down as one of the best Internet Marketers in History. I am a loyal follower, my friend!

Marshall Sylver – (The Millionaire Maker™) who helped give me a Bigger Vision during my stay at Prosperity Palace and becoming a great friend.

David D'Arcangelo – for giving me my very first shot "LIVE" in front of a large crowd on-line and trusting in my ability to learn and then teach. Plus some of the most sound financial advice I have ever received. Our paths will cross again, I am sure of it, my friend!

Mike Filsaime & Captain Lou - what can I say .... *"The Marketers Cruise" changed my life!

There are so many people I have missed, however, I would like to thank YOU! Especially the people who have watched me over the past couple years and seen me grow as a Person and an Internet Marketing Coach. This book is because of YOU and this book is FOR YOU!

*Note: any resources I mention in this book can be found at:

http://WebcastRiches.com/resources

Author's Preface

Webcasting has truly changed my life. It is amazing when I look back over the past two years how this industry and technology has changed. I cannot imagine where it will be in another two years. The best thing is YOU can be part of it.

Today, I make more than a full time income, working from home, doing two (one hour) live webcasts per week.

Now, that sound like I only work two hours per week, but, I do not want to mislead you here.

There is a lot more to webcasting than simply firing up the webcam and logging into your webcast room, however, it is one of the easiest "money making" and fun activities you can add to your marketing toolbox.

I do want to warn you that webcasting is almost like a drug. Once you start doing it, it can get addicting!

I am not ashamed to say that I have become well known and one of "THE" go to guys on the internet when it comes to live webcasting software, presentations, instructional techniques and more importantly profiting from live webcasts. I have helped some of the biggest names on the internet, behind the scenes, become successful and extremely profitable with their live internet broadcasts.

During one webcast I helped set up, we sold nothing and actually "gave" a $197 digital product out for free, yet, over the weeks to follow sold over $250,000.00 worth of products. The best part is we are still making residual income to this day from this well planned one hour webcast.

I would dare say that I have helped produce $3 Million Dollars or more in sales over the past two years.

I wish I had kept better track, but, when I started doing live webcasts I was having so much fun and just like time flies when you are having fun, so does keeping track of the numbers. I had no idea that it would be so popular, profitable and inexpensive. I certainly did not think I would be writing a book about live webcasting.

Technology has made it so anyone, anywhere in the world with a high speed internet connection can become a "live internet broadcaster" and profit. I like to call it LIVE WEBCASTING!

Because of people like Joel Therien (CEO and Founder of *GVO Conference) and Mike Potvin (*GVO's Director of Marketing), along with their strong team of in house developers, the simple to use webcasting technology & web based software are within reach of anyone, no matter what their fnancial situation is.

You can purchase a great webcasting room of your own for about $1/10^{th}$ of the cost that you could two years ago and with more bells and whistles than you will ever use. It is like having your own internet TV station 24 hours a day 7 days per week.

You are reading the first in what I hope to be a series of books on webcasting. As technology and marketing techniques change we hope to have many books on webcasting in several niches.

Okay, enough about me.

Let's jump right into the real reason you purchased this book.

"To Learn and Profit from Live Webcasting"

- Mark Call

Contents

Introduction

The world of business and commerce never stands still.

It changes constantly, and as people involved in business on a daily basis, we go with the flow and adapt to these changes as they happen.

Over the past couple of decades, perhaps the biggest single change to hit the business world has been the advent and subsequent phenomenal growth of the Internet as a business tool.

The net is a truly global platform that allows your message to travel from one side of the world to the other in the blink of an eye, thereby making international trade a reality even for the smallest of businesses.

In many ways, the net has brought about a true commercial revolution by giving every online marketer or business owner an almost unlimited ability to market and sell.

And yet, and yet…

Isn't it also true that in the modern business world, we are all increasingly bogged down with things that don't have anything with making money?

For instance, no matter what your business is, I'll bet that you have more meetings, training courses and seminars to attend than ever before.

They are probably valuable and they do help you to improve but the sad fact is, meetings and the like eat into your precious marketing time and ultimately reduce the profitability of your online sales efforts.

As an example, there may be traveling involved when you attend a presentation or seminar. Travel costs both time and money. It's time when you could have been marketing your products and services too.

Then there are conference calls and a million and one other things that need to be attended to.

All of these things render your daily activities less efficient at a time when achieving exactly the opposite is more important than ever before.

Nowadays, it's a fact that in increasingly competitive markets (i.e. all business environments), efficient organizations survive and thrive while the less efficient go to the wall.

You sure as heck don't want to be in the latter category, right?

So, how can you take advantage of the inarguable benefits of attending training, collaborating with customers or even training others without the waste of resources that is inevitably associated with doing so physically?

Welcome to what I genuinely believe is the 'wonderful world of webcasting'.

1. What is webcasting?

What it is...

A webcast (or a webinar as it is alternatively known) is a broadcast that you conduct over the internet. This could be a group meeting of pretty much any type, such as a training session or online meeting.

For marketers however, the primary attraction of webcasting is that it enables you to sell your products or services to a group audience without ever having to leave your office or home.

Another thing that differentiates a webcast different from other forms of online broadcasting is the degree of interactivity involved.

It's a two way thing in other words, as you can present your content and your audience can respond to it in real time.

Any project where two or more people need to collaborate and work together can be handles courtesy of the power of webcasting.

Through the net, attendees from anywhere in the world can be brought together in one 'conference room'. Depending on how you conduct the meeting, everyone who takes part can see, hear, send text chat and participate with others who are in the room at the same time.

Furthermore, you can share slide and Power Point presentations, show screen shots from your computer (still or active) and even conduct instant polls or ask your attendees to complete a survey, all as part of the webcast!

In short, there is nothing that you could do in a 'real' meeting that you cannot do in an online webcast.

Now, the specific details of exactly what you can do when conducting a webcast will be at least partially dictated by the software you are using.

I will highlight my favorite webcasting software later and explain the exact reasons for liking it so much. For now, suffice to say that the software I recommend includes all of the benefits of webcasting that have already been mentioned, and many more besides.

Why include webcasting in your marketing mix?

If you're reading this, I'm guessing that you have never used webcasting to promote your business before.

However, it is a fact that the use of webcasts is booming as more and more businesses begin to appreciate the advantages of conducting meetings online.

If you compare webcasting with the way you would conduct a 'traditional' meeting, it is abundantly clear that webcasting has many advantages. It is indicates why you should be getting in on the 'webcast wave' right now.

To begin with, incorporating webcasting in your marketing mix allows you to communicate with and sell to a truly global audience.

If you are promoting an product or service, webcasts enable you to do so to prospects everywhere without boundaries or limitations.

Furthermore, the fact that your webcast is a virtual meeting means that your expenses in terms of time and money are limited. You do not have to travel to meet your prospects and you are able to present to a large number of them at the same time.

Now, of course, webcasting is not the only way that you can present information about your products and services to a mass global audience.

For instance, building a mailing list of prospects that you send information to on a regular basis has long been a favored tactic of online marketers, and it still works very well.

Webcasts nevertheless have many advantages over more traditional marketing methods.

To begin with, e-mail marketing is not immediately interactive.

While an e-mail message might persuade a subscriber to take a specific action, it doesn't happen instantly and there is no element of a 'back and forth' real-time exchange of information as there would be with a webcast.

It's also a fact that the written word appeals to human intellect and emotions, but only through one channel or medium.

Your e-mail message gets read and if the words on the page are powerful enough, they prompt the reader to take action.

Watching and participating in a video webcast is however a completely different experience.

Video persuades your audience to watch (i.e. it engages their eyes, which is crucial as most humans are 'visual' creatures) and their ears.

A video meeting invites them to play an active part in an event and your audience is far more aware of your tone and body language too.

Based on extensive research, webcasting experts suggest that it is not only big businesses that benefit from staging webcasts either.

On the contrary, personal experience has shown me that small and medium-sized business operations can benefit every bit as much as global conglomerates.

In effect, if you work in a massive office tower or on your own in your spare bedroom, it makes no difference when it comes to conducting successful and profitable webcast events.

Anyone can do it, and the tools and resources that I recommend are priced to ensure that producing successful webcasts is eminently affordable too.

But perhaps the greatest thing about marketing using webcasting is that it is not only your business that benefits from your decision to do so.

Webcast marketing is great for your prospects and clients as well.

For example, the interactive nature of webcasting means that if they have a question or query, you can answer it immediately. This is great for them. They want the answer now and a webcast is perfect for providing it.

It is also tremendous for you too of course.

Questions and queries often become significant buying objections if left to hang.

If however an attendee poses a question that is dealt with immediately, the potential objection is nipped in the bud. Hence, it becomes much more likely that you'll land a sale.

The 'group' nature of a webcast produces another advantage for your attendees (and for your business as well).

Even if an individual participant does not think of a specific question, others are likely to ask it for them.

Consequently, every member of the group has a far more detailed and in-depth understanding of the subject matter (your product for example) than they might otherwise have.

They have also got to 'know' you far more naturally than they could via almost any other method of online communication.

There is therefore a degree of trust already established that might take weeks with better known communication channels such as e-mail.

They know about your product or service and they have got to know you.

Perhaps not surprisingly, this makes it more likely that they will buy from the webcast – you've already 'pushed the right buttons', after all.

This is one reason why a successful webcast can generate hundreds of dollars in sales revenue from just a few hours work.

The bottom line is simple – if you are not including online webcasts in your marketing mix, you are missing a terrific opportunity to expand your business and your profitability.

This is true irrespective of the kind of business you own or operate.

Webcasting is easy to do and does not need complex technology or advanced presentation skills either.

As I suggested earlier, running a successful webcast is something that anyone can do. And the sooner you get started, the sooner you'll see results.

2. Why video is the way to go...

As suggested earlier, there are different types of webcasting, with what you do being dependent on the software or podcasting system that you use.

The simplest form of webcasting is audio only. In this case, your audience can only hear you although they might be able to see your computer screen as well.

To an extent, audio webcasting is a little like interactive radio. Your webcast attendees can listen in and participate but an element of the experience of being 'part of something big' is inevitably lost.

On the other hand, video webcasting enables you to take full advantage of the genre far more effectively. They can see you and communicate with you, thereby enhancing the impact and effectiveness of your broadcast.

In my experience, online video conferencing always produces superior results to working with an audio-only model.

When the spoken word was the only game in town, it was fine but the effectiveness of it has been completely superseded by video webcasting.

There are many reasons why video always works better, some of which are fairly obvious while others might be less so.

Most obviously, if people can see you, they get to know you.

People do business with people rather than with a faceless 'business'. Moreover, they like to do business with people they like and know.

Less obviously, with the growth in the availability of cost-effective webcasting software, broadcasting video is rapidly becoming the accepted norm.

Consequently, if you create audio-only webcasts, you risk being seen as old fashioned and out-of-date, someone who is perhaps less willing to invest in your business.

The final factor in favor of video webcasting is the overwhelming popularity of online videos nowadays. The fact is that the modern net user expects their information and entertainment to be presented in video format.

Consequently, nothing else even comes close to video content in terms of giving your potential prospects what they want, the way they want it.

As an example of the popularity of online video content, YouTube.com is the third most popular website on the net with 24 hours of video materials uploaded to the site every minute.

There are in excess of 2 *billion* YouTube views every day which is nearly twice as many people as tune into the 3 main prime-time networks in the USA combined.

There is no doubt that online video is the new TV, and if you don't use it, you're falling behind the game.

3. Why webcasting is so profitable

There are many reasons why setting up a webcast for prospects in your business can be one of the most profitable decisions you will ever make.

In this chapter, I'll highlight some of the main reasons why you can make so much money (irrespective of your business) from webcasting.

Attendees must register

When you invite people to a webcast and they decide to register, you get their e-mail to enable you to confirm the invitation and remind them about the event shortly before it starts.

As most experienced online marketers know, a 'hot' prospect mailing list is second only to a customer list in terms of future revenue in the bank.

Consequently, even if the prospect registers for your webcast and does not subsequently attend (as will happen), you have at least got a degree of commitment from them. They are on your subscriber list, giving you the ability to sell to them as many times as you want to in the future.

It levels the playing field

It doesn't matter whether you run a multinational company or work on your own, webcasting is exactly the same. Sure, the big company may be able to afford flashier software or a super-trendy system but at heart, you and they are in precisely the same situation.

This essentially means that webcasting is one form of marketing where the size of your budget is fairly irrelevant.

If you create a webcast production that is engaging, compelling and persuasive, you can generate as much business as you want no matter how well-established or new to online business you are.

Find out what prospects and customers want...

One of the greatest advantages of webcasting is the element of instant interactivity because as the name suggests, it works both ways.

This means that you can present your product or service on a webcast and you'll very quickly have a feel for how your prospects and/or customers are reacting to what you are doing and offering.

This is vital feedback which you would not be able to collect in any other way. As a result, you are able to improve your business in response to what you learn when webcasting, thereby enhancing your future profitability.

For instance, my recommended video webcasting software would allow you to see the members that are in your webcast 'conference room'.

You can therefore monitor how many of these people stay with you, how responsive they are and generally keep track of other 'reaction' metrics.

By doing so, you quickly establish whether the product is a good match for this audience or not, whether the particular style of webcasting that you are using is a 'hit' or not and so on.

This is information that you can use to improve your webcasts in the future which in turn improves the profitability of what you do.

Customer loyalty

Webcasting enables you to get to know your clients and quickly gain loyalty from them while doing so.

As suggested, webcasting allows you to learn what your customers and prospects want or need. Give them what they need, and they will be loyal to your business.

If 'your' people know that you provide top-quality information every time you broadcast an event and that the products you recommend or produce are top-notch, they are unlikely to take a chance by going elsewhere.

Effective use of time

I would recommend that your webcast presentation should be restricted to one hour or thereabouts. There should also be time for a 'Q & A' session but overall, the event should never run for more than two hours.

When you frst start producing webcasts, you'll need to do some planning and some practice before going live.

Even so, it still only takes a few hours from beginning to end (including your practice time), in return for which you can generate thousands of dollars of sales.

Webcasting is therefore an extremely time-efficient and a profitable way of marketing your business, products or services.

What is more, as you acquire more experience, the planning and practice stage becomes easier and even less time consuming, whilst the quality of your webcast improves at the same time.

Hence, webcasting is a very effective way of making large amounts of money in a short period of time and this becomes increasingly true the better at it you are.

Relatively limited competition

It doesn't matter what market or niche you operate in, I am confident that very few of your competitors actively include webcasting in their 'regular' marketing mix.

Firstly, many of them are not even aware of just how powerful webcasting can be (if they have encountered the concept at all).

It's a sad but true fact that the majority of online marketers stick to the same old, same old marketing methods without ever 'looking up' to see if there are any exciting new ideas on the horizon.

Secondly, for many, there is something vaguely daunting about hosting their own webcast. They think that it is too difficult, something that needs professional presentation skills without which the whole thing will fall flat.

For them, it is much easier (and safer) to stick with marketing tactics with which they are already comfortable rather than taking a perceived risk by becoming a webcaster.

Once again, this is very short term thinking because they are letting a superb marketing opportunity pass them by.

Moreover, it is also incorrect too.

The fact that a webcast is 'live' means that your attendees do not expect a perfect presentation. In fact, you can lose where you are in the proceedings, continually 'erm' and 'aah' but your audience will not care as long as the information you're presenting has value to them.

Imperfection is an integral part of human nature and webcasts (particularly those that focus on sales) are all about people on both 'sides' of the event getting to know and become comfortable with one another.

Consequently, even if you don't look perfect in front of the camera, it doesn't matter. If you have an accent, it's irrelevant as long as it's not completely impenetrable for anyone outside of your region.

If you have a tendency to break out in fits of giggles, don't sweat it unless it begins to disturb the flow of your presentation.

Like I said before, anyone can do this while anyone who doesn't is leaving a lot of money on the table.

For one reason or another, the majority of your competitors do not use webcasting in their marketing and they will not do so in the foreseeable future either (unless they read this book of course).

The competition is therefore eminently beatable because in many markets, it's almost non-existent.

4. Planning your first webcast event

Especially in the early days of your webcasting career, detailed and careful planning is absolutely essential.

While experience brings the ability (and probably the contacts) to put a successful webcast together without too much work in advance, you've got to learn to do it right when just starting out.

As you already know, there are several reasons why I believe video webcasting is the way forward in this business. Perhaps you've taken these ideas on board, fully understanding the advantages of video but you are concerned about the cost of top quality software?

If so, I'm going to introduce you to the perfect solution with an excellent video webcasting program that costs less than $9 a month. Cost should not therefore be an issue.

So, let's assume that you are going to produce your first video webcast, and you've got the software already.

The very first thing you must do is learn how to use it properly.

This is essential because understanding how to broadcast your event well in advance of being called upon to do so is one potential worry or hiccup out of the way.

Next, you must decide what you want to achieve with your webcast.

For instance, is it about introducing your business to new prospects or selling your products or services to existing 'warm' prospects? Perhaps you're promoting someone else's product as an affiliate?

Alternatively, do you want to host a webcast to generate new leads or as a way of enhancing your service to your existing customers?

Of course, there is no reason why you cannot webcast to achieve all of these objectives, but you cannot do so all at once.

You must have a specific focus or target for every webcast you produce, a very precise target at which everything you do is aimed.

If on the other hand you try to cover too much in one session, you are asking for frustration and failure. It will only become confusing if you try to do too much, so make sure you have a goal and that you stick to it.

Okay, with your webcasting software in place and a specific purpose decided upon, you are ready to move forward by putting together a detailed plan of how you are going to achieve your webcasting goal.

Why 'content is king'...

It's maybe one of the most clichéd and hackneyed phrases in online marketing as a whole, but it's 100% true that when it comes to achieving success in webcasting, 'content is king'.

It is the content of your broadcast, the quality, the value and usability of the information that you provide which ultimately dictates how successful you are as a webcaster.

You can be a complete beginner and yet you'll still achieve your objectives and start to build a top-rate reputation if you present attendees with exactly what they want or need when they turn up for your webcast.

So, this is the question that you must answer before doing anything else.

What do people in your market or niche want or need?

Do you know?

If so, great − you already have the basic content ideas for your webcast. All you need to do now is develop these ideas into a workable script.

If however you do not know what people in your business need, you must find out before diving in to this thing. There is absolutely no sense in *guessing* what they want because doing so is a recipe for an empty webcast conference room.

To find out what people need, start by asking your list subscribers.

Tell them that you're considering a series of webcasts and ask what they would like to hear or watch.

To begin with, ask them what the one big question about your business that they would most like an answer to is. Find out what other elements of achieving success in your industry they find most perplexing or difficult.

Question whether there are any prominent industry leaders or experts that they would like to see or hear interviewed.

If you have a responsive list of subscribers already, asking these questions quickly enables you to create an excellent framework around which you can build your webcast.

You have the questions that people in your niche are asking so by including them as well as the answers that they need, you address the conversation that is going on inside their heads.

Doing this is incredibly powerful because 'getting inside their head' creates an immediate empathy, a bond between you and your attendees that subconsciously persuades them to take whatever action you want them to take. If you are trying to land sales, you will if you 'connect' with people or if you are attempting to train them, they will learn so much faster when you are inside their head.

Getting the information that enables you to do this is easy if you have subscribers that you can ask, but what if you don't?

Well, finding what you need requires a little more work, but it can still be done.

Start by looking at the most popular forums in your niche, those that are the most active with lots of members.

Monitor the conversations because you are likely to see some questions that are repeated time and time again, albeit in a slightly different form. These are the most pressing questions that people in your market need answers to.

Get involved in the most active forums and start adding valuable content (e.g. your own threads, and responses to those of others) as a way of establishing trust and rapport with other members.

You can ask questions yourself. Try asking other members what their biggest worries fears, concerns or problems are and you'll get the information you need.

If you build a network of targeted followers using social networking sites like Twitter (http://twitter.com/), Facebook (http://www.facebook.com/) or MySpace (http://www.myspace.com/), use the social access you have to ask questions that point you in the right direction.

By combining the networking ability of these sites with your forum research, you have access to information that is very nearly as good as that which you would get from list subscribers. Of course, the most complete answer would be to combine all of these tactics.

One final option would be to create a short questionnaire, post it to a webpage with a small giveaway prize for anyone that responds before advertising your survey.

Use an online classified ads program like Google AdWords (the most expensive option) or even advertise with Facebook to find out what people want or need.

Having done so, all that remains is to work what you have discovered into a script that you can webcast (either alone or with a co-presenter) to provide the information that people in your market need.

Invite a guest

Surveys indicate that one of the most effective ways of achieving webcasting success is to invite a guest expert to participate in your event.

Assuming that this individual is well-known in your niche, having a guest to help you immediately increases the number of exciting, willing attendees.

There are several reasons why this works so well.

To begin with, an expert has expert things to say!

I know it sounds self-evident but unless you can claim the same status yourself, they have the knowledge and experience that your prospects and/or customers are really interested in.

They might not turn up for you (until you become well-established), but they will attend for a presentation that involves an industry 'superstar'.

The fact that you can get this person to help you out is however a feather in your cap, an indication that you might be a 'coming' guy or girl in your market. A guest expert on the webcast therefore attaches immediate credibility to you and your business.

If there are two or more people on your webcast, it spreads the workload too.

Your audience came to listen to your expert and not you.

Consequently, your job is to 'pump' him or her for high-quality information or 'secrets' and then let them get on with it because in this way, you tend to get them most out of them.

At the same time, you must control the conversation because you only have a certain amount of time available. No matter how prominent your expert is, do not allow them to dominate or take over your presentation.

Stay in control, keep an eye on the time and if they are taking over your event, do not hesitate to step in to wrest control from them.

One question that you may have is how do you find such experts to help you? The answer is, go back to the most popular forum sites in your niche because that is probably where the authority figures hang out.

When you do so, you should quickly come to recognize those that other members seem to look up to. These are the people that you should start to build a relationship with through active participation to enable you to invite them to be part of your webcast events in the future.

When you do so, remember that they are only going to help you if you can give them a good reason to do so. They want to know what giving up an hour or two of their precious time will do for their business, so you must be able to answer this question before contacting them.

For example, if they have a new product launch coming up that you can promote as an affiliate, it's a perfect time to ask them to appear on your webcast. They are looking for every possible opportunity to promote their product, so your offer is likely to be gratefully accepted.

At the end of the day, even the most widely recognized experts in your market will help you if you present a strong enough argument about why doing so will benefit them when you first contact them.

The importance of practice...

One very effective way of retaining control of your presentation is to have a script prepared in advance. If you are running the webcast on your own, the script is just for you whereas you should script on both sides of the conversation if you are inviting a guest.

Once you have your script, organize a 'dry run', a practice session which enables you to establish how your script fits your allocated time.

If you have a guest on the webcast, see if you can arrange at least one run-through with them, even if you have to do it online using a service like Skype.

If however they cannot make it, find someone who can 'stand in' for them so you have a decent idea of how your script stacks up time wise.

And of course, a practice session or two enables you to work on your own timing and your confidence. The first time you webcast, you will be nervous which tends to make you speak more quickly than usual. Practice helps to calm the nerves and get rid of this problem.

Even so, I would recommend having a few 'extra' questions tacked on to the end of the script just in case you finish too quickly for one reason or another. In this way, you ensure that you don't get 50 minutes into your one-hour webcast and dry up!

Promote, promote, promote...

It doesn't matter how engaging your topic or how illustrious your star guest is, nobody will turn up for your webcast if they don't know about it.

You must promote your event and do so well in advance and in as many different ways as possible too.

There are many ways you can promote your webcast but if you have a mailing list of opted-in subscribers, they are your first target.

Begin an automated e-mail sequence at least two weeks before the event and 'drip-feed' the information in an effort to build suspense and excitement.

For example, say you are in on the launch of a brand new online marketing product as an affiliate. Start dropping hints about the webcast to introduce the product and the benefits of it but do so very slowly. If you can get the product creator involved with your webcast, so much the better.

Tell them that you are hosting an invite-only webcast for just 50 or 100 people in order to emphasize the exclusivity of your event.

This encourages them to register early which is helpful as it allows you to gauge the level of interest and enthusiasm.

Make sure to tell them how to sign up for the event and also instruct them to do so as well. Crazy as it sounds but just adding something like 'click this link and sign up now' often increases attendance by a significant margin.

It's therefore something that you should always remember to do.

After this, gradually increase the tempo and intensity of your mail campaign, stressing that they will miss out in a big way if they do not attend. All the while, you must constantly remind them that it is an invite-only event and that there are only a limited number of places available.

Finally, make sure that you send a series of 'last minute reminder mails' to get as many people as possible on the call.

If you have a list of loyal customers already, this tactic should fill your webcast 'conference room' without any difficulty.

But even if you do not have a mailing list, there are other ways of drawing attendees to your event.

For instance, I have already mentioned the fact that you can build and communicate a list of niche targeted followers and friends using social networking sites such as Facebook, Twitter and MySpace.

Start doing this now because these people will be perfect to invite when you begin webcasting, but you cannot afford to leave building a list of targeted followers and friends to the last minute.

Instead, get started with a Facebook Fan Page and an active Twitter account for your business right now as these lists will be invaluable in the future.

They haven't got time to waste...

Planning or scripting a webcast is a little like developing sales page copy when you are selling a product on the net.

Your prospect (or attendee) wants to get to the point as quickly as possible whereas your objective is to build the excitement and anticipation to a climax that is so powerful that your audience cannot help but take the action you want them to take.

There is therefore a bit of a mismatch here. You cannot build sufficient excitement in 10 or 15 minutes, whereas your attendees do not want to listen to you (even if you have a prominent guest on the panel) all night.

This is why you cannot afford to let your webcast run on too long, with a one-hour presentation being just about ideal for both parties.

Of course, this has to be an hour of high-quality, valuable content but as long as you can satisfy this requirement, most of your attendees will be happy with a 60 minute presentation.

In addition, you need time for dealing with questions and queries. If possible, I would recommend setting aside as much time as your audience wants after the presentation has finished to work through a Q & A session.

Some webcast hosts invite questions as they go along. Avoid this if you can by announcing that the Q & A session follows the presentation. Otherwise, the webcast content easily becomes fractured and the flow is interrupted, lessening the overall value of your presentation.

Demonstrate the value of your product...

One of the major advantages of using video webcasting is that it enables you to demonstrate the merits of any product you are promoting or selling.

This is much more powerful than simply telling people about what your product or service has to offer.

As the saying goes, 'seeing is believing'. It is far easier to convince prospects to buy a product that they see in action than to get them to take their credit card out after you tell them how good it is.

For example, if you are promoting a software program, it would be easy to create a video that you include in your webcast to demonstrate how it works and how effective it is.

You could demonstrate a physical product if this is what you sell rather than a digital product.

If for instance you sell vacuum cleaners, you show people how good they are by throwing dirt on the floor before making it disappear or you could show people how well your food mixer works if this happens to be your product.

Similarly, if you're promoting a network marketing opportunity, there are several ways you can 'demonstrate' your product with a webcast.

As an example, if you're trying to attract new members to your network, you can show them how it works and how much money you are making from your business.

Alternatively, you can demonstrate how your attendees can become better marketers by demonstrating the successful methods you use to recruit others by teaching them how to find a prospects 'hot button' for example.

In short, no matter what your product or service is, a webcast gives you a great opportunity of demonstrating the benefits of it live. Nothing makes selling easier than a convincing demonstration, so this is a huge advantage.

Ask questions and conduct polls

As suggested, webcasting enables you to connect with your customers and prospects almost directly.

You should therefore make the most of the opportunity by finding out more about them with questions and by conducting polls as part of the webcast experience.

Not only does this furnish you with invaluable information, it also ensures a lively and engaging event with lots of audience participation and feedback.

On the other hand, not inviting your attendees to take part is a mistake that erodes the effectiveness of your webcasting activities. If they do not feel comfortable about participating, attendees can feel marginalized and peripheral which is clearly not what you want.

So, make sure that you ask questions occasionally and use the 'poll' utility within the webcasting software to keep your attendees fully engaged.

Survey participants afterwards

In the same way as you use questions and quick polls during your webcast, prepare a short survey in advance that attendees are asked to complete afterwards. This again helps you to know what your participants thought of the webcast and how you can do an even better job in the future.

5. Free or paid for?

Another question that you need to give some thought to is whether you are going to allow prospects to participate in your webcast events for free or whether you are going to charge them an 'admission fee'.

There are several factors to consider when deciding which approach is best.

To begin with, it is likely that free webcasting e is the only realistic option until you become reasonably well-known. Most prospects will be skeptical of paying for a webcast that is presented by someone they have never heard of. Trying to charge would therefore kill your event.

If of course you have a top industry expert webcasting with you, someone who is a household name in your business, it might be a different matter. The fact that they are excited by listening to or watching your guest overrides the fact that they don't know you in this case.

Apart from exceptions like this however, you can't charge until you acquire a high-quality reputation, after which, you might be able to.

The question is, should you do so?

There are two schools of thought on this.

On the one hand, if you do not charge an 'entrance fee' for your webinars, you will have lots of prospects that accept the invitation. If on the other hand you charge for attendance, it reduces acceptances significantly.

The problem with free webcasts however is that while lots of people say that they are going to attend, an awful lot don't do it. They'll forget or find something better to do or in some cases, they never genuinely intended to participate in the first place.

If it's free, it's very easy to accept and then not come to the ball.

After all, what have they lost by doing so? Nothing, right?

It's also an unfortunate fact that for many, free equals no value.

Even if the quality of your webcast content is top-notch, the perception that some prospects have beforehand is the opposite because it's free.

Thus, you have another reason why free may not always be the best way.

On the contrary, I know of webcasters who charge a fee for exactly these reasons.

They do not want 1000 people who accept an invite to a free event where only 50 turn up. They would rather have just 100 that accept a paid-for invitation because they know that 90 or 95 will attend when they have paid to do so.

Asking people to pay to attend an event is also a good way of convincing people that the quality of the content is top class.

If the presentation is not top quality, you wouldn't be charging for it, right?

It might not be true but it's the way people think.

It doesn't have to be a lot but asking people to pay sometimes attracts a bigger crown to a webcast event, especially if you are creative about how you structure your entrance fee 'schedule'.

For example, I know webcast hosts who use forums like the Warrior Forum - the leading online marketing forum at:

http://www.warriorforum.com

to invite people to their events.

They charge $1 for the first ten people to accept, $2 for the next ten, $3 for the ten after that and so on. In this way, they encourage people to sign up early and ensure that almost everyone who says they will attend do so.

The other reason why charging for your webcast often works is because asking for money gets a genuine commitment. It implies a higher level of need for information or answers on the part of the attendee as well.

Even if you only ask a dollar or two, the fact that someone is willing to spend money to hear what you (and/or your guests) have to say tells you that they have not chosen to come out of idle curiosity.

Instead, they need what they believe you have to offer and as any experienced online marketer will tell you, 'desperate' people are willing to spend whatever it takes to solve their problems.

The fact that people have shown a genuine desire to attend your event by spending money suggests that selling an entry-level product is likely to be fairly easy in this situation.

However, selling a $29 or $49 is just the start in many cases, the first level of real financial commitment to your business.

Assuming that the product is high quality and provides some of the answers they are looking for, a successful entry-level webcast makes it far easier to sell high ticket products or services from future webcasts.

As an example, there are millions of people all over the world who are desperately trying to make it in network marketing.

Many of these people have spent a lot of money in their past efforts without a great deal of success and they really need to achieve success sooner rather than later.

Say you offer a webcast where you have a prominent expert in network marketing as your guest.

He (or she) has an entry level product at $49 with a 'platinum' level one-to-one training course (and 'bootcamp') for $497 as an upgrade option.

To go from a $49 product straight up to $497 would usually be too big a leap in one step for many.

However, an additional webcast series that emphasizes the benefits of the 'upgrade' will generate sales because these are people who really need success, and the Platinum product is hopefully be the key to the door.

The reality is that convincing people to pay to attend your webcast is not always easy, especially in the early days.

However, once you are in a position to persuade potential attendees of the value that you offer, the money making potential of paid events can be significantly higher than that of the free version.

There are of course other factors that need to be taken into account when considering whether charging for your webcast event is realistic or not. Alongside your own experience and reputation, the industry you work in and the purpose of your proposed webcast many also have an influence.

Only you can answer where you stand in this respect, but be careful not to prejudge the issue.

You might think that you could never charge for a webcast or you might be 100% certain that you can. What you think or believe does not however matter one iota.

The only way you can ever know for certain is by asking the market what they want by trying different approaches and ideas.

6. Making money from webcasting...

I have just highlighted how you might be able to charge attendees a fee for your webcast events.

However, until you are widely recognized as a leading expert who can charge premium prices for attendance, you are never going to make much from attendance fees.

Hence, the question is, how do you make money from webcasting?

There are several answers to this as you can make money both directly and indirectly from your webcasting efforts. Let's look at the two in turn.

Direct webcasting money makers

As suggested previously, the first (and possibly most obvious) direct money maker is to use webcasting to sell your own products or services. The fact that you can use a webcast to demonstrate the effectiveness or efficiency of your product is a very simple way of boosting sales.

Alternatively, you can use webcasting as a highly effective way of leveraging your affiliate marketing efforts. You sign up as an affiliate for a particular product or service and then present information about your promotion to a mass audience on a webcast.

This is a particularly profitable tactic if you have the original product creator as part of your event presentation team as highlighted earlier.

Exactly the same principle applies if you own and run an online (or even off-line) shopping resource. You demonstrate your products and make sales as a result of doing so.

If you are a network marketer, there are two distinct elements of your business that you can sell with a webcast.

Firstly, you have products to sell. Everything you have read in the previous few paragraphs therefore applies to you.

Secondly, you can present the benefits of membership of your network to a large audience of prospects very easily and quickly with webcasting.

Elements of the membership program that might be a little difficult or long-winded to explain in writing can be explained far more simply with the aid of visual tools – white boards, project diagrams, network models etc. – using video to demonstrate how things work.

Your webcast content can become a high-quality product in and of itself too.

For example, if you record the event, you can release it as a standalone information product.

If you sell the recording as a digital download on its own, you'll make money. If you add an e-book transcript of the recording, the price you charge for product has just gone up.

The value climbs even higher if you convert the presentation into retail quality DVDs

(see http://www.kunaki.com/)

that are delivered to the customer's door and higher still if the e-book is converted into a print version that is also delivered.

Another option is to convert your webcast materials into a training course, a membership site or system where you charge a regular monthly fee for access to your training materials.

This is a tremendous option because you sell the membership idea just once and yet collect an ongoing fee week after week or month after month.

What is more, these are superbly well targeted prospects for other products and services that you market in the same niche.

Membership sites present a great opportunity for cross promotion, hence you have members who are paying month on month and buying other products or services from you every so often as well.

Indirect money makers

It should be obvious that the more widely known you are as an expert, the easier it becomes to sell your products and services.

Consequently, anything you can do to improve your market visibility and share is going to indirectly improve your bottom line cash flow at one and the same time.

Webcasting is one of the best ways of raising your profile, rapidly taking you from wherever you are now to a position of authority in your market.

And don't forget, this is leveraged prominence that we are talking about.

You can get your message to 100 or 1000 people with exactly the same amount of planning and effort as you would if you were talking to just one prospect.

And of course, the more prospects there are who know you and what you do, the louder the buzz surrounding your business becomes.

No matter what market you are in, you inevitably face competition.

We all do no matter what kind of business we run. What is more, the competition only ever gets tougher.

Using webcasting gives you an advantage over almost of those whose businesses are ranged against yours because they are not webcasting.

What is more, my own experience taught me that webcasting success is something that grows with increased knowledge and experience of what works in your marketplace.

Consequently, if you include active webcasting in your marketing mix from this point on, you will be much further along the learning (and earning) curve should your competitors start webcasting in the future.

If you already dominate the webcasting marketing 'niche' in your business by then, it will be very hard for them to knock you out of the #1 position.

7. Simple success guidelines...

I guess that for some, a number of the simple success guidelines that I highlight in this chapter might be blindingly obvious.

Even so, I make no apology for including them for one very simple reason.

They may be obvious but I have seen far too many new webcasters fall down because they did not pay sufficient attention to these basic requirements. Obvious perhaps but nevertheless, attention to detail is utterly crucial if you are to succeed.

The first minute

When you open your webinar, make sure that there is something on the screen that tells your attendees they are in the right place. If they hit a blank screen or a wall of silence, it may create sufficient uncertainty to convince them that they are in the wrong place.

Beyond this, if you are talking over (say) a Power Point slide with the webcast title during this critical first minute, make sure that you are positive, upbeat and enthusiastic. These first seconds set the tone for the whole event so you must make it as energetic and lively as you can.

Make sure that you get straight into telling your audience how they will benefit by staying with you. You have less than 20 seconds to convince them that you have something of value for them, so be sure to tell them what it is as quickly as possible.

If you have a guest on the presentation, introduce them to establish exactly why they should be listened to, but stay in control and keep it short.

Remember that the frst minute of your presentation sets the tone for everything else that follows. You must therefore make sure that the event starts off with a bang if you want to keep your audience numbers up.

Keep it interesting

It does kind of go without saying that you must strive to keep the webcast interesting. To do this, you should analyze your presentation from the audience point of view to see whether what you are thinking of doing works.

Remember that everything you say and do will be viewed by attendees from the 'what's in it for me?' perspective. Everything you are thinking of including in your webcast must therefore be analyzed from this same angle.

The content must be interesting and engaging, while the language you use and the style of presentation should be the same.

For instance, bring emotions into the language you use because emotional language is far more persuasive than bland or neutral words.

You don't 'like' something, you 'love' or 'adore' it. You don't get 'a little bit annoyed', you 'get mad' or you 'rage'.

Your body language is also very important too. If you are upbeat, energetic and clearly enjoying yourself, your audience members cannot avoid getting caught up in the same feelings of energy and enjoyment.

The opposite is also true. If you are downbeat and clearly not enjoying yourself, attendees will recognize it and reflect the same feelings.

Of course, you may be a little nervous presenting your webcast but don't make it look like you are on your last walk to the gallows.

Instead, there is nothing wrong with saying that you feel a little nervous but you can put a positive spin on it even when you do so.

For example, you could suggest that it is the presence of such an 'eminent and world-famous expert' in the room that is making your nervous or it's the fact that you have such a huge audience on the call.

The bottom line is, if some element of your planned presentation is not interesting and does not 'give' to your audience, it has no place in your webcast.

Proofread and proofread again...

Make sure that you go over your script in minute detail to confirm that everything makes sense, is spelt right and gets your message across as succinctly and as powerfully as possible.

What I would do is write a draft script and then put it to one side while I go about other things for a couple of days. Coming back to the script after a break is often the best way of seeing the mistakes and errors that you have made as well as elements of your presentation that can be improved.

Do this two or three times, all the while attempting to edit the content for maximum impact from as few words as possible.

When you have something close to what you believe to be the final draft, get someone else whose judgment you trust to go through it for you.

Ask them for any improvements that they can see, making it clear that you are willing to accept what they say as constructive criticism and that you're not going to get upset or annoyed.

Having an independent third party assess your proposed presentation may not always be the most comfortable or pleasant experience. Even so, the chances are high that the improvements will be more than ultimately justified by the results.

Professional and prompt

Your webcast must start on time every time, with no exceptions. Anything else is unprofessional and disrespectful to attendees that turn up on time.

It is inevitable that you will sometimes have problems, particularly once you have become a regular webcaster.

For example, some would-be attendees might have connection problems but there is nothing you can do (or should attempt to do) about this once the set start time for your presentation arrives.

You can of course open the meeting 10 or 15 minutes early to help anyone having problems overcome them, but once the anointed hour arrives, you can delay no longer.

Another problem that you may encounter is connection problems when you have a guest who is appearing on your webcast over the net.

You must therefore have a fallback 'plan B' that can be rolled out in the event of your guest not being able to attend at all.

To create this emergency plan, simply modify your original two-way script into something that makes sense coming from just one person.

Audience convenience

I've already suggested that you should remind everyone who has agreed to be on your webcast shortly before the event that it is about to take place.

Do this a couple of hours before hand by e-mail and then again, one final time approximately 15 to 30 minutes before you are due to start. Would-be attendees will be on your mailing list after accepting the invitation, so contact them by e-mail.

In addition, make sure that you pump out reminders using your social networking resources such as Facebook, Twitter and maybe even Skype.

Reminding people is just one element of making attending your webcast as easy as possible, albeit a very important one.

Another element of convenience is to conduct the webcast event at a time that is likely to be convenient for most.

Given that your broadcast is global, there is no single time zone that is most convenient for everyone although in the evening Eastern Standard Time (say, 8PM or 9PM) is a pretty popular time to start.

Of course, if your initial webcast it is a success, there is no reason why you cannot run the same event at a different time to enable those who couldn't make it first time round to attend.

Finally, if there is information in the event that is not easy to take a note of in a hurry – website URLs for example – include them on a fixed screen at the end of the presentation and/or send them out by e-mail later.

Above all else...

More than anything else, you must provide your attendees with as much quality and value as you possibly can. The information presented during the webcast must be valuable enough to justify their attendance while anything else that is offered should also provide a 'bonus experience'.

For example, if you are offering a product for sale, do so at a discount price that is only available to your audience members.

Similarly, if you are presenting training materials, you could create a series of bonus videos that are free to anyone that subscribes to your mailing list.

Remember, webcasting success is always predicated on providing maximum quality and value to attendees. Focus on providing what your audience most need 100% of the time, and you'll never go far wrong.

8. Webcasting mistakes to avoid

Having stated that 'you'll never go far wrong' at the end of the previous chapter, I'm just about to show you a few very effective ways of doing so!

All joking apart, these are mistakes or errors that it is fairly easy but extremely dangerous to make. You must therefore be aware of and avoid making them at all costs.

Not standing out from the crowd

The majority of your competitors are not currently include webcasting in their marketing arsenal.

Some of them may do so however, and they might be quite good at it. They are targeting the same market as you. You are therefore in a battle for audience attention.

On top of this, your prospects are being bombarded with thousands of marketing messages every day. You have to rise above this 'noise' as well if you are to become a webcasting success story.

Consequently, you must avoid falling into the trap of doing the same as everyone else.

While it is extremely tempting to observe what others do so that you can duplicate those efforts (particularly if you are following someone who is very successful), you should not become a 'webcasting clone' of anyone.

Instead, you must do everything you can to stand out from the crowd, to be someone that is recognized as different and ideally better.

As an example of how you might achieve this, start by integrating all of your marketing efforts under one brand name and image. Everything that you produce should then be appropriately branded so that popular awareness of your brand and style gradually (or – even better – rapidly) increases.

The brand style that you choose is going to be with you for a very long time. You should therefore put time into designing a brand and an image that works from the outset.

In other words, your brand must truly represent you and your business with a broad appeal for potential clients and customers in your marketplace.

Remember, it's all about benefits...

Do not fall into the age old trap of focusing your webcasting on the features of your product because no one cares about features.

Instead, everything you present should be benefit related, stressing to them how their life will be improved by taking advantage of whatever you offer.

As an example, no-one cares that the vacuum cleaner you are selling has a 5HP electric motor. What they care about is the fact that the increased cleaning power means that they can cut cleaning time in half, allowing them more leisure time with friends and family.

If there is a guest involved...

When you invite a guest to any event that you are going to webcast, do not make the mistake of assuming that their agenda is exactly the same as yours. On the contrary, they probably have very different objectives to you.

As an example, if your guest has recently produced a brand-new product, they would love to spend the whole hour talking about it.

On the other hand, while the 'price' of inviting them on is giving them 5 or 10 minutes to talk about the product, do not allow them to dominate proceedings.

You must therefore script what you want them to do and say. In addition, be certain that they fully understand (and agree to) what is going to happen.

It's your event, so you must retain control.

Be prepared...

I've already highlighted how important it is to prepare your webcast event in detail the, but what happens afterwards is equally important.

Sadly, it is very easy to become so obsessed with 'the main event' that everything else becomes secondary, ignored until the webcast is done.

This is a big mistake because right after the event is the time when your audience members are most receptive to whatever you present to them.

If they get an e-mail from you reminding them about the benefits of your product immediately after the event, they will open it. If however you wait a week or two, they've almost forgotten that they ever attended.

In short, you must have your follow-up marketing campaign in place in advance of staging your webcast.

As far as possible, the campaign should be automated – outgoing e-mail messages loaded to an autoresponder for example – because all being well, you'll be snowed under with sales activity after a successful webcast.

Not having support in place...

With the webcasting software that I will introduce a little later, it is perfectly possible to handle the whole webcasting process single-handedly.

Nevertheless, there is a limit to what one person armed with a software program can do, especially when unforeseen problems or glitches arise.

This is especially true if you are not technically inclined or intimately acquainted with the more intricate workings of the net.

If your system goes down 5 minutes before you are due to start, you are in a major hole and it's probably one that you cannot climb out of alone.

For this reason, it is useful to have assistance at hand, aides that can step in if or when things go wrong.

In fact, even if things are perfect for you, assistance is still very useful as there will be would-be attendees for whom things are not going nearly so well. They cannot hook up to your presentation and they'll be onto you by e-mail or Skype asking for your help.

You'd be powerless to provide assistance in this situation. Once again therefore, help is necessary.

This does not necessarily mean that you need to employ full-time support staff.

Instead, you will fnd suitably qualified freelance staff from websites like V-Worker

http://www.vworker.com

to help you on an 'as-and-when' basis.

These are experts that you can pay for two or three hours of support work whenever you need them.

Hence, you have a sufficiently large team to ensure that your webcast goes smoothly without having to pay a full-time salary for a job where they are needed only occasionally.

9. Where to next?

You need software

In the same way that succeeding as a webcaster without a support team could be difficult, you must have the right tools for the job as well.

To begin with, you need webcasting software to enable you to broadcast your message to your audience when you are ready to do so.

There are many different webcasting software programs and systems available, but in my opinion (and that of many other top-flight online marketers), the system you should be using is GVO Conference.

There are many reasons why I believe that this webcasting system is going to one that becomes massively popular in the next few years.

To begin with, the GVO Conference software has full video webcasting capabilities. Perhaps surprisingly in this day and age, a lot of the major competitors do not.

Secondly, the price is outstanding, with a 50 seat conference room of your own (for life) costing just $8.97 a month.

The people behind GVO are top-quality marketers in their own right with many, many years experience in this business. They know what it takes to market and make money online and offer you a great opportunity to do so with GVO Conference.

The software is truly cross-platform as well. Unlike some of the other options, attendees can use GVO Conference on their Mac or a Linux driven machine as well as on those machines that use Windows.

A lot of online marketers prefer Mac (in particular) to Windows. This is therefore an important consideration even if you use the ubiquitous Microsoft operating system.

Basically, GVO Conference is being positioned as an enterprise grade webcasting solution that combines all of the features (and benefits) of other leading solutions for a fraction of the price they charge.

Simply put, if you want to market with webcasting, you need the software to do the job. GVO Conference is set to be the best of the best, and there'll never be a better time to get involved. To see full details, visit:

http://www.webcastriches.com/gvo

Conclusion

There's a ton of killer webcasting ideas and knowledge in this book but they're only a part of the story behind why I've been so successful with and made so much money from webcasting.

You see, I've been around online marketing a long time and I know how it works.

I know that not everyone who reads this book or looks at my website is an action-taker and that some will – sadly – do nothing with the huge amount of knowledge they have been given in this book.

I make no secret of the fact that I want to work with action-takers, the people who are willing to take their destiny into their own hands and work to achieve success.

So, I've kept some of my best 'secrets' back to include them in my brand-new Webcast Riches training program.

This is a program that enables anyone to learn the real inside 'nitty-gritty' of making money from webcasting and (obviously) one that I would thoroughly recommend.

It is however a program for action takers, one in which I've included pretty much everything that I've ever learned about webcasting.

Webcast Riches is therefore exactly what the name suggests it should be – a complete blueprint to making a ton of money on the net with webcasting.

If making thousands of dollars by staging fun events live on the net sounds like it is for you, then I'd urge you to head over to my site at:

http://www.WebcastRiches.com

This is not an opportunity that will be open forever because there are only so many people I can work with.

If you want to see what it is all about, I really would recommend visiting now.